UNBROKEN GROUND

Healing from Hidden Wounds
& Building Unshakeable Self-Worth

DR. ALANA SHARPS

Book Creation & Design
DHBonner Virtual Solutions LLC
www.dhbonner.net

ISBN for Paperback: 979-8-9931883-0-0
ISBN for eBook: 979-8-9931883-1-7

Published in the United States of America

CONTENTS

"Your decision today will define your tomorrow."

-Anonymous

PREFACE

I spent sixteen years in an emotionally and verbally abusive marriage, being conditioned to conform to a man whose main objective was to control me through intimidation, threats, rage, and gaslighting while appearing to be charismatic and the perfect husband and father to friends, family, and the world around us.

Our relationship didn't start this way. My husband was a very loving and caring man who treated me with respect while we were dating. It wasn't until we married that things changed; he became someone I didn't recognize. He belittled me, called me explicit names, and constantly criticized me. He became enraged and threw things when he didn't get his way. He began to isolate me from my family and friends through manipulation and intimidation tactics. He listened to my phone conversations, often becoming enraged by what was being said, and read my texts to see with whom I was communicating.

I began to think five steps ahead, "walking on eggshells," while trying to anticipate his mood. I took the blame for things I knew were not my fault, just to keep the peace. He told me it was my fault he mistreated me; I believed him without challenge. I felt alone... imprisoned, unheard... lost.

I spent most of my marriage trying to find the man I dated in the person I was married to, but that man didn't exist. I finally picked up the pieces of my self-esteem and found the courage to leave the marriage after numerous prior attempts. In the days that followed, the mental fog lifted. I began to see the impact that our marriage had on our children. In my fight for survival, I couldn't see the struggle my children were having with their father's antics. They were also learning that it was okay to have someone who claimed to love us bully, berate, insult, and humiliate us.

I'll never forget my oldest son's words as we sat at the kitchen table in our tiny two-bedroom apartment two weeks after my escape. "Mom, you seem so happy now." You see, my son always saw me in a trauma response...conforming, taking blame, and being put down. He didn't know Mom as a strong and happy woman in a healthy relationship.

What I experienced in my marriage was coercive control, a form of intimate partner violence: Acts of intimidation, threats, and humiliation to control and maintain power over another person by eroding their autonomy and self-esteem.

A few years ago, I wrote my best-selling memoir, *Was it*

My Fault? An Abuse Survivor's Story and Guide for Navigating Narcissistic Red Flags, detailing my story. Since its release, I've grown, healed, and supported many men and women with similar struggles. What I have learned, over time, from consulting with my divorce coaching clients is that we all feel powerless, overwhelmed, defeated, and traumatized after years of chronic emotional abuse. Our brains have changed... they are broken from the abuse we endured in our intimate partner relationships. Our nervous systems are still in high fight-or-flight because we're often in the middle of high-conflict child custody disputes or co-parenting with someone who would rather be a counter-parent than do what is in the best interests of the children.

The legal system labels our legal cases "high conflict" due to the legal chaos and the amount of time it takes to reach an agreement or court-ordered settlement with a high-conflict individual, the high-conflict individuals being our ex-partners. Typically, they refuse to negotiate, collaborate, or do what is in the best interest of their children: someone whose sole purpose is to win, punish, and maintain control over their victim.

We thought we were finally free when we left our relationships, only to find out that the abuse transitions to post-separation abuse, which comes in the form of:

- Counter parenting
- Harassment
- Stalking

- Weaponizing the children
- Financial abuse
- Legal abuse
- And so much more

We're so used to defending ourselves to our ex-partner that we continue the same behavior post-separation, often responding emotionally instead of strategically. Our brains are traumatized and easily triggered. We may cry while speaking or speak out inappropriately when our abuser spews false truths during mediation or court proceedings. Only this time, the courts are involved; our words can be misconstrued as the words of a crazy person when, in reality, these are trauma responses from survivors who are continuing to be abused during the family court process. They are the words of a survivor trying to protect themselves and their children from further harm, survivors trying to do the right thing while also trying to heal, evolve, be good parents, and rebuild their lives while still experiencing abuse.

This book is for the emotionally beaten-down survivor to guide them on their healing journey to rebuild their mental rigor, self-confidence, and autonomy while continuing to experience or recover from the experience of emotional abuse.

INTRODUCTION
EMOTIONAL ABUSE

> *"Emotional abuse is often a misunderstood form of trauma, perhaps the most damaging type of abuse, that leads to long-term consequences for adults (Heim et al. 2013)."*[1]

Emotional abuse is a form of psychological abuse. It's a pattern of behavior used to control a victim through isolation, manipulation, gaslighting, intimidation, shame, and fear that results in significant emotional harm. Unlike physical abuse, emotional abuse targets a person's mental and emotional balance, eroding their self-esteem, autonomy, and sense of self-worth over time.

---

1. Heim CM, Mayberg HS, Mletzko T, Nemeroff CB, Pruessner JC. Decreased cortical representation of genital somatosensory field after childhood sexual abuse. *The American Journal of Psychiatry*. 2013;170(6):616–623. doi: 10.1176/appi.ajp.2013.12070950.

Emotional abuse is mental warfare. It can occur during childhood, in the workplace, in intimate partner relationships, or in friendships. We often normalize maltreatment in adulthood if we grew up with a parent who chronically emotionally abused us during childhood, making us unable to identify that what we are experiencing in future relationships is emotional abuse. The treatment is familiar since it is how we were treated during our developmental years.

In this section, you will learn how to recognize emotional abuse and its long-term effects on a person's mental and physical health.

Emotional abuse is more psychologically damaging than physical abuse, leaving deep and lasting scars in a person's brain. Prolonged emotional abuse can result in emotional trauma, including anxiety, chronic depression, complex post-traumatic stress disorder, and autoimmune disease. Recognizing and addressing it is vital for a victim's recovery.

Types of Emotional Abuse and Recognizing the Signs

There are many types of emotional abuse, but some are used more than others in relationships. The most common types are:

- *Verbal Attacks*: Constant criticism, name-calling, bullying, berating, and insults. The abuser belittles the victim's appearance, capabilities, achievements, and anything else that makes the victim who they are, making them feel worthless.

- *Manipulation and Gaslighting*: The abuser distorts reality, lies, or twists facts using pressure and persuasion to control a victim. Gaslighting or "crazy making" is a common technique used to make the victim question their memory, judgment, and even their reality.

- *Isolation:* The abuser isolates the victim from friends and family in an effort to control who they see or talk to, limiting their social interactions and support network. The isolation reinforces the victim's dependence on the abuser.

After I married my husband, he occupied all of my time, discouraging me from seeing my friends. My family lived five hours away, so seeing and spending time with them was limited. I went out one evening to see a girlfriend I hadn't seen since my marriage. When I returned home, my husband made me feel guilty for going out, stating, *"GOOD mothers don't need to spend evenings out with friends."* He continued to belittle and harass me for the rest of the night. He used a fear that I had shared with him during dating--of failing at being a good mother to my children--to manipulate, control, and isolate me from my friends.

- *Intimidation:* The abuser uses threats, shouting, and other aggressive behaviors to create fear and intimidation in the victim. The abuser may also use non-verbal tactics, such as glaring, throwing objects at or near the victim, and destroying objects.

- *Emotional Blackmail:*[2] The abuser manipulates the victim's emotions to get what they want through guilt-tripping, blaming the victim for the abuser's problems, and threatening to harm themselves or others if the victim does not comply with their demands.

- *Control and Dominance:* The abuser seeks to control every aspect of the victim's life, including their choices, behaviors, and feelings. This can manifest as dictating how the victim should dress, wear their hair and makeup, or behave.

- *Shame and Humiliation:* The abuser publicly or privately humiliates the victim, making them feel

---

2. Emotional Blackmail: When the People in Your Life Use Fear, Obligation, and Guilt to Manipulate You by Susan Forward, PhD

embarrassed and ashamed. This can involve bringing up past mistakes, mocking the victim, or spreading false rumors about them.

- *Ignore and Neglect:* The abuser will give the victim the silent treatment, ignore their needs and feelings, or withhold affection and support as a form of punishment or control.

Walking on eggshells in an attempt not to enrage someone and to keep the peace is also a common sign of emotional abuse. I consistently did this in my marriage: Trying to determine my husband's moods by his body language and tone of voice so as not to set him off.

A victim of emotional abuse may not recognize that they are being abused. The tactics used by an abuser are used subtly over time, slowly eroding the autonomy and self-esteem of the victim. You recognize that something is not quite right and often feel low and have feelings of guilt, shame, or anxiety around the abuser; however, you can't put your finger on why you feel that way. You are left in a state of confusion, believing you are the cause of the maltreatment. Your abuser will reinforce this negative self-perception by reinforcing that the treatment is either caused by something you didn't do or something you did that they didn't like. Emotional abuse is not something we are taught in schools or discussed among friends or family unless someone has experienced it. Even when discussed, it can be difficult for outsiders to understand our experience since they cannot identify with it. When I was experiencing emotional abuse in my marriage, I didn't know I was being abused. I just knew my husband often made me feel inadequate with his belittling remarks. I continuously tried to appease his every need while the bar of satisfaction rose daily.

I repeatedly explained the cycle of abuse (I didn't know that's what I was explaining at the time) to multiple marriage counselors; they never picked up on it, leaving me feeling as if I was the cause of my husband's mistreatment. I described the highs and the lows: how he was loving and caring one day and demeaning the next. It was a consistent pattern. Only one counselor picked up on it. It was toward the end of my marriage when I was so mentally worn down that I didn't believe her when she said my husband was a narcissist.

To be honest, I didn't fully understand the definition of a narcissist at the time, so I dismissed her assessment as "that's not my problem" when she, indeed, was one hundred percent correct. It wasn't until I escaped my marriage and educated myself on narcissism that I realized what I had experienced for sixteen years. Everything finally made sense.

Increasing awareness of the warning signs of emotional abuse can help you recognize and seek support for yourself or others, such as friends and family, who may be experiencing emotional harm.

Reflect on your current and past relationships. Are there any that exhibit patterns of emotional abuse? Have you experienced any of these emotional abuse tactics in a relationship? How did it make you feel?

The Long-Term Effects of Emotional Abuse

Emotional abuse can have severe long-term effects, such as:

- Low self-worth and self-esteem
- Difficulty trusting oneself and others
- Chronic anxiety and depression
- Memory problems
- Serious impacts can include complex post-traumatic stress disorder and autoimmune disease.

You may experience feelings of helplessness, shame, and guilt due to believing the emotional abuse you have endured is your fault. It also doesn't help when abusers often tell victims that they are being abused because they didn't do, act, or say something correctly. I was consistently told in my marriage that everything was my fault, including my husband's extramarital affair. Something he "chose" to do.

You may struggle with trust issues and have difficulty forming healthy relationships. It is hard to trust again when your trust has been aggressively betrayed. It is important to seek support from mental health professionals and engage in therapies that focus on healing from trauma when you have escaped living with your abuser. Trying to heal and rebuild yourself while living with your abuser doesn't work. I tried it and failed miserably. My body continued to suffer due to chronic stress.

Emotional Abuse Statistics

- 48.4% of women and 48.8% of men in the U.S. have experienced psychological aggression by an intimate partner in their lifetime[3]
- Women who earn sixty-five percent or more of their households' income are more likely to be emotionally abused than women who earn less than sixty-five percent of their households' income. [4]
- Women experiencing emotional or psychological intimate partner violence are significantly more likely to report poor physical and mental health

---

3. Black, M.C., Basile, K.C., Breiding, M.J., Smith, S.G., Walters, M.L., Merrick, M.T., Chen, J., & Stevens, M.R. (2011). The National Intimate Partner and Sexual Violence Survey (NISVS): 2010 Summary Report. Atlanta, GA: National Center for Injury Prevention and Control, Centers for Disease Control and Prevention.
4. Kaukinen, C. (2004). Status compatibility, physical violence, and emotional abuse in intimate relationships. Journal of Marriage and Family, 66(2), 452-471.

and to have more than five physician visits in the last year.[5]

- Emotional or psychological abuse is a stronger predictor of PTSD (Post Traumatic Stress Disorder) than physical abuse among women.[6]

The Importance of Recognizing Abuse and Building a Safety Plan

Emotionally abusive intimate partner relationships can be dangerous and unpredictable. When you recognize abuse is occurring in your intimate partner relationship and you have found the courage to leave, it is crucial to have a safety plan in place. Identify potential danger signs that may cause emotional abuse to escalate to physical abuse. By recognizing the warning signs, you can proactively plan for safety and take action when needed.

Trust your gut instincts. They are there to protect you. Don't push them down. If it doesn't feel right, it's not right. When I planned to leave my marriage, I informed my close friends and family as a safety net. If needed, I had a place to go should things escalate before I could move out.

5. Coker, A., Smith, P., Bethea, L., King, M. & McKeown, R. (2000). Physical health consequences of physical and psychological intimate partner violence. Archives of Family Medicine, 9(5), 451-457.
6. Dutton, M.A., Green, B., Kaltman, S., Roesch, D., Zeffiro, T. & Krause, E. (2006). Intimate partner violence, PTSD, and adverse health outcomes. Journal of Interpersonal Violence, 21(7), 955-968.

I stayed vigilant and on guard, paying attention to my husband's mood swings for potential signs of physical danger. It took me two months to finally be able to move out. It was the most stressful two months of my life, fearing what my husband might do as retaliation for my leaving him. Every day during those two months was an emotionally terrifying experience that I never want to go through again.

In addition to family and friends, you can also seek help from local shelters, hotlines, or legal resources. For safety, always inform someone you trust prior to planning your escape. Interview trauma therapists. Trauma therapy can help survivors process their experiences and develop strategies to cope and escape an abusive situation.

Emotional abuse is an insidious form of abuse with long-lasting effects. Recognizing the signs of emotional abuse in intimate partner relationships is crucial. Once you recognize the signs, you can formulate a plan to leave and begin the recovery process. If leaving is not possible due to financial or other reasons, informing friends, family, domestic abuse hotlines, your church, or someone else you trust about your current circumstances is important. You never know when the abuse will escalate to physical abuse when the abuser feels they have lost control. Develop a safety net for your own safety and time of need, don't be afraid to ask for help, and lean on your support system.

EMOTIONALLY ABUSIVE PARENTS

> *Emotional abuse may be the most damaging form of maltreatment, causing damage to a child's developing brain, affecting their emotional and physical health, as well as their social and cognitive development.*[1]

E motionally abusive parents abuse their children similarly to how they emotionally abuse their significant others. Children, on the other hand, are not equipped to handle the manipulation, gaslighting, and control tactics of the abuser. They are also struggling with the dilemma of parents who are supposed to love, care, and

---

1. Heim CM, Mayberg HS, Mletzko T, Nemeroff CB, Pruessner JC. Decreased cortical representation of genital somatosensory field after childhood sexual abuse. *The American Journal of Psychiatry*. 2013;170(6):616–623. doi: 10.1176/appi.ajp.2013.12070950.

support them, not harm them. This makes the parental relationship very confusing for children who only want to be loved and cared for and to please their parents.

Emotionally Abusive Behaviors in Parenting

Manipulation: Emotionally abusive parents often manipulate their children to get what they want by guilt-tripping, fear, or playing the victim.

Gaslighting: Emotionally abusive parents make their children question their own thoughts and reality by denying past events, telling the child they are lying, contradicting the child's experiences, or blaming the child for all of their adult problems. This can severely undermine a child's confidence and sense of self.

Children end up confused by the gaslighting, making them feel like a failure or inadequate, needing to strive harder to earn the love and approval of the emotionally abusive parent. My oldest son was the scapegoated child. He was blamed for everything that went wrong in his father's life and everything that went wrong in the home.

Emotional Neglect and Devaluation: Emotionally abusive parents neglect their children's emotional needs and devalue their feelings and achievements. This can come in the form of ignoring the child's feelings, dismissing their accomplishments, or showing favoritism (scapegoat and golden child phenomenon).

My daughter was the golden child, the favored child who, at a very young age, was the emotional support system for her father. She was too young to be an adult's shoulder to cry on. She was also the child who could do no wrong in her father's eyes, regardless of her behavior. The lack of correction she received for improper behavior was imposed twofold on her brother, the scapegoat.

Impact of Emotional Abuse on Children

The impact of emotional abuse on children and teenagers will manifest in different ways. Similar to adult victims of emotional abuse, children live in survival mode, trying to appease, please, and steer clear of aggressive mood swings from the emotionally abusive parent.

They often develop anxiety, anticipating the next unprovoked rage, wanting to avoid it at all costs, and trying to conform to whatever the emotionally abusive parent wants or needs. Children can lack self-esteem from the constant criticism, demeaning remarks, and subliminal messages thrown at them by emotionally abusive parents.

When children grow up in emotionally abusive homes and are passed back and forth as assets during divorce and child custody settlements, it's important to pay attention to the changes in their behavior, recognizing warning signs that signal intervention is needed. Younger children often have difficulty vocalizing what they are feeling and experiencing, and teenagers will often internalize. In both instances, therapy is needed.

You can't control what happens in the emotionally abusive parent's home; however, you can control what happens in your home by showering your children with love, validating their feelings, and providing quick access to care. Here are some warning signs of emotional abuse in younger children with an emotionally abusive parent:

- Developmental delays
- Learning disabilities
- Wetting pants or bed wetting (enuresis)
- Withholding bowel movements
- Speech disorders
- Anxiety
- Difficulty sleeping
- Weight fluctuation or obesity
- Overly compliant or defensive
- Inappropriate behavior for their age

Children may also have emotional outbursts, be overly assertive, talk back, and throw temper tantrums after spending custodial time with the emotionally abusive parent. When children return from time with the emotionally abusive parent, allow for 24 hours of detox (low stimulation, slow-paced day, time to calm down and talk, express emotions, but with boundaries (i.e., if angry).

Older children, preteens, and teenagers, on the other hand, express their mental challenges with emotional abuse in many ways:

- Develop skin conditions or other health issues
- Weight fluctuation or obesity
- Eating disorders
- Extreme emotions
- Anxiety
- Depression
- Difficulty sleeping
- Social anxiety and withdrawal
- Overly compliant or defensive
- Destructive or antisocial behavior (e.g., cutting or not leaving the home)
- Suicidal thoughts or behaviors (ideation)

My youngest son was ten when I left my marriage in 2018, and my daughter was fifteen. My youngest grew up seeing his father rage and yell when he didn't get what he wanted, while we all lived together in the marital home. Due to that experience, he became a people pleaser, scared to make a decision without understanding what other people want. For example, if I ask my son, "What would you like for dinner tonight?" His response is always, "What do you want for dinner?" He bases his decision on my response to avoid offending me.

My daughter, on the other hand, internalized the emotional and physical abuse she witnessed and endured. She believes everything that happened in the marital home was her fault and that she is a failure in everything she does if it is not perfect, which causes extreme emotions, severe anxiety, and depression. She often controls her food intake, sometimes withholding food for extended periods or engaging in binges; she has trouble sleeping and has nightmares of her father harming her. The year of her sixteenth birthday, she struggled with suicidal ideation.

A sign I missed during her early development years was the withholding of bowel movements at the age of four, for which we saw numerous specialists to determine if it was a physical issue. It wasn't until the latter years that I learned this was a sign of distress in children. My daughter is still on the road to recovery. We celebrate every small win, no matter how small it is. My oldest son, who endured the most abuse in the home, has low self-confidence, depression, gets overly defensive in conversation, has social withdrawal, and has difficulty determining a path in life.

> *As children, we want our parents to love us and take care of us. When our parents don't do this, we try to become the kind of child we think they'll*

love. Burying feelings that might get in the way of us getting our needs met, we create a false self —the person we present to the world. When we bury our emotions, we lose touch with who we really are, because our feelings are an integral part of us. We live our lives terrified that, if we let the mask drop, we'll no longer be cared for, loved, or accepted.[2]

Have you observed any of these signs in your children? If you have, what was the impact of that observation (initially, as a victim yourself, you may not have the clarity to see it happening to your own children, or there may be resistance to accepting the cause of the behavior)?

It is extremely important to pay attention to your children and the warning signs signaling they need help. I missed many signs while I was married due to being in my own struggle for survival. Looking back on my marriage, the signs were there that my children were struggling as well. Once I escaped the marriage and was able to focus on the children, I made their mental health a priority. My children are still recovering from the emotional abuse they experienced, even as adults.

When children spend custodial time with an emotionally abusive parent in shared custody situations,

---

2. 4 Ways Childhood Emotional Trauma Impacts Us As Adults, July 13, 2017 | Haven Staff

their basic needs of love, having an identity, emotional support, validation of feelings, and being able to express themselves are stifled. A healthy parent shows love through quality time and respect, making the child feel safe, and doing what's in the child's best interest. The parent meets the needs of the child for healthy development.

Establishing a Safe and Supportive Environment

A physically and emotionally safe environment is vital for children who are spending significant custodial time with an emotionally abusive parent through a child custody agreement.

The healthy parent should maintain a safe space where the children are free to express themselves without fear of judgment or retaliation; they are respected and free from fear, anxiety, and manipulation. Children thrive with routines. Maintain a set dinner time, bath time, and bedtime routine. Even though children may fight the routine at times, the consistency and predictability of the routine help to create a safe space for them. Also, involve your children in planning activities to give them a sense of control and autonomy. One of my daughter's biggest complaints about living in an emotionally abusive home was her lack of autonomy and feeling in control of her own life.

Building Trust and Open Communication

Trust and open communication are foundational pieces of a child-structured, supportive environment. Children need to know and trust that they can come to you with their feelings and concerns. Never interrupt or dismiss a child's concerns. Once children feel that you are not listening to them and validating their concerns, they will shut down and no longer express their feelings to you.

> *How can you encourage your children to express their feelings and concerns openly?*

Ways to Foster Trust and Open Communication

The very basic needs your children require to thrive and grow in life will not be met by an emotionally abusive parent. Therefore, it's your responsibility to meet those needs when the children are with you.

Respect Your Children. We all deserve respect regardless of age. Treat your children as the human beings they are, with their own thoughts, feelings, and needs. My oldest son never received the respect he deserved from his dad. His dad felt entitled to treat him as a possession that needed to "fall in line or else" rather than a human being.

Validate Your Children's Feelings. Ask your children questions. Ask them how they feel. Teach them to express themselves and be one with their feelings. Suppressing their emotions is not healthy, and they will carry that behavior into adulthood. My daughter still struggles with "feeling" after suppressing her own emotions for so many years.

Offer Your Children Choices. Allow your children to feel that your love is genuine and not dependent on which choice they make. Emotionally abusive parents do not know how to show love. Their attention to their children is dependent upon what they will receive in return. Show your children you will love them regardless of their choices or their behaviors.

My youngest child still struggles with making independent choices after growing up in a household where the "wrong" choice was met with anger and rage.

Healthy Boundaries. Educate your children on healthy boundaries and respect their physical and emotional boundaries. Teach them by example. Your children should see you exercising healthy boundaries as well. If your child has a bad day at school, is upset about what happened when you pick them up from school, and expresses not wanting to talk about it, respect their boundary by not forcing a conversation. Let them know that you love them and are available for them to talk to when they are ready.

Having Compassion. Use mistakes as an opportunity for learning and growth. Teach your children that mistakes happen instead of inducing shame or belittling them for making a mistake.

Getting Upset. Use healthy forms to express and model displeasure with children (take a walk, deep breathing exercises to calm down, or get upset at the behavior and not at the child, for example). Do not resort to retaliation, passive-aggression, or the silent treatment. These expressions of anger will be experienced by children during their custodial time with the emotionally abusive parent.

Rupture and Repair. Take accountability for your actions and repair fractures in your relationship. It is never too late; children, even adult children, offer you the opportunity to repair what has been done.

Active Listening. Practice active listening with your children instead of listening to respond. Allow your children to be seen and heard. Make eye contact, avoid interrupting, reflect back what they say, and ask open-ended questions to encourage them to share more. Fully concentrate, understand, respond, and remember what the child is saying. This teaches children that their thoughts and feelings are valued.

Encourage Independence and Autonomy.
Emotionally abusive parents thrive on control and dependency. Counteract those behaviors by helping your children develop a sense of independence and autonomy. This will empower them and build their self-esteem.

Healthy Coping Mechanisms. Teach your children healthy ways to cope with stress and emotional pain. It is essential for building their mental toughness. Encourage your children to draw, paint, act in plays, play sports, play an instrument, or practice mindfulness activities as a coping mechanism for what they are experiencing with their emotionally abusive parent. My daughter loves to paint. It is the activity that calms her mind the most.

Emotional Resilience. Teach your children how to believe in what they see and what they hear to help manage gaslighting from the emotionally abusive parent. Teach them to trust their gut instincts and that adults are not always right in what they say and do. You can perform role-playing scenarios with your children to help them recognize gaslighting. Encourage activities, such as journaling or drawing, for self-expression.

Self-Esteem and Confidence. Build your children's self-esteem and confidence through positive reinforcement. Encourage their interests and talents. Be proud of them for the things they are excited about. Building your children's self-esteem and confidence involves recognizing and celebrating their strengths, encouraging their interests, and providing opportunities for success. Highlight the importance of positive reinforcement and avoiding comparisons with others.

Seeking Professional Support

There may come a time when children need additional support from mental health professionals to address the impact of emotional abuse. Therapy can provide a safe space for them to explore, talk about their emotions, and heal. A therapist can also provide additional coping mechanisms that children can carry into adulthood.

Encourage Them to Build Their Own Support Systems

Your children may not always want to come directly to you for support. They may feel more comfortable expressing themselves to a trusted outside source. It's important for your children to have their own support systems, including trusted adults and peers they can turn to for help and guidance. Encourage your children to participate in extracurricular activities that are of interest to them so they can form friendships and connect with supportive adults, such as coaches, teachers, or mentors.

Navigating Co-Parenting Challenges

Co-parenting with an emotionally abusive ex-partner can be incredibly challenging, but it is possible to develop strategies that protect your children and minimize conflict. Here are some effective co-parenting strategies to help you navigate this difficult terrain:

Stay Focused on Your Children's Best Interests. Keep your interactions with the emotionally abusive parent business-like and focused on what's best for your children. Avoid getting drawn into emotional conflicts, and always prioritize your children's needs.

Maintain Consistency and Stability. Children thrive on consistency and stability. Create a structured environment with predictable routines to give them a sense of security. Be sure to offer them as much advance notice as possible (if you can) when there is a change in structure.

Communicate Through Neutral Channels. To reduce conflict, use neutral channels for communication, such as text, email, or co-parenting apps. This helps keep interactions focused and documented. Co-parenting apps like Our Family Wizard (OFW) facilitate communication and scheduling while maintaining a record of interactions. OFW is a popular app recommended by family courts.

Handling Manipulation and Gaslighting. Recognizing and countering manipulative behaviors from the emotionally abusive parent is crucial for protecting yourself and your children. Develop strategies to counteract manipulation, such as sticking to facts, avoiding emotional responses, and setting firm boundaries.

Discuss the Emotionally Abusive Parent's Behavior with Your Children. It's important to discuss the emotionally abusive parent's behavior with your children in an age-appropriate manner without badmouthing. Help them understand the behavior without creating confusion or fear. Focus on the behavior rather than the person when discussing with children, providing reassurance and support.

Legal and Professional Support. Seeking legal advice from an attorney and emotional and strategic support from a divorce coach will help protect your children's best interests and give you an understanding of your rights and the resources available to you.

Documenting Interactions. Keep detailed records of interactions with the emotionally abusive parent to show patterns of bullying, emotional manipulation, guilt-tripping, etc., for legal proceedings. Documentation should include dates, times, incidents, and any evidence collected via voicemails, emails, texts, videos, etc. Use Google Drive, a journal, or a Word document to keep records organized.

Maintain Emotional Boundaries. Emotional boundaries are essential when dealing with an emotionally abusive ex-partner. Protect yourself from emotional manipulation and maintain your mental durability. Practice self-care and seek support from friends, family, or a trauma therapist. Learn to recognize when to step back and protect your emotional health.

Dealing with Co-Parenting Conflict. Conflict is inevitable in co-parenting with an emotionally abusive parent, but how you handle it can make a significant difference. Stay calm and focused, avoiding escalation of the situation. Respond to emails and texts after taking time to process the information to avoid emotionally responding and saying something you will regret later.

Navigating co-parenting challenges with an emotionally abusive ex-partner requires patience, strategic planning, and a focus on your children's mental and physical wellness. By implementing effective strategies, maintaining emotional boundaries, and seeking professional support, you can create a more stable and supportive environment for your children.

Setting Boundaries with Emotionally Abusive Parents

Establishing clear boundaries with the emotionally abusive parent is essential to protect your children *and* yourself from further emotional harm. This includes setting limits on interactions and communication. Allowing them to communicate with you verbally opens the door for further emotional abuse and gaslighting.

I learned this the hard way and suffered emotional turmoil. Limit communication to co-parenting applications, email, and text messages. A strong parenting plan with predetermined boundaries and parallel parenting clauses is another strategy to help maintain your sanity.

Responding to Allegations

Emotionally abusive parents love to throw allegations around to see what will stick in a legal setting. All of the allegations will involve making the healthy one appear neglectful, as a difficult co-parent, or crazy. As much as you feel the need to respond immediately to every single text and email received from the emotionally abusive parent, you don't have to unless it's an absolute emergency. Don't take the bait. Emotionally abusive parents thrive on making you emotionally respond to their nonsense. By emotionally responding, you are falling into their trap.

Breathe, take a step back, determine how you will factually respond, and then reply. If needed, take a day or two. Have a friend or family member read your response before you send it to ensure it is not accusatory or emotionally charged.

> *Reflect on the boundaries currently in place with your ex-partner. Are they effective?*

Self-Care for the Healthy Parent

I can't express enough how important it is to take care of your basic human needs, such as food, sleep, and activity. If your body is worn down due to a lack of nourishment and adequate rest, you won't be in a good frame of mind to support your children or be strategic in dealing with the abusive parent. So, taking care of yourself is critical for supporting your children emotionally.

If you don't take care of your physical and emotional self, you won't have the mental capacity or armor to support your children when they are in need. Self-care involves managing stress, maintaining physical health, and finding time for relaxation and enjoyment. Therefore, incorporate self-care activities into your daily routine, such as walking, exercise, meditation, hobbies, and spending time with friends and family. Make self-care a priority, even when it feels challenging. Your body and mind need it, and your children need you to be mentally healthy.

Long-Term Consequences of Emotional Abuse

Childhood emotional abuse[3] includes constant criticism, put-downs, and rejection. Emotionally abusive parents stifle children from expressing anger or sadness, impacting their emotional development. Childhood emotional abuse can lead to emotional pain, anxiety, depression, self-criticism, low self-esteem, suicidal ideation, and difficulty forming stable and trusting relationships.

---

3. www.psychologytoday.com/us/blog/tech-support/201611/the-enduring-pain-childhood-verbal-abuse

The long-term impact of emotional abuse on children includes difficulties with self-worth, trust issues, and challenges in forming and maintaining healthy relationships. It can also lead to serious mental health issues if not addressed. So, understanding emotional abuse and its impact on children is the first step toward providing the necessary emotional support and the development of interventional plans in the form of therapy and support networks.

Recognizing the signs of emotional abuse in children and taking proactive steps to help mitigate the effects of abuse helps to foster a healthier environment for developing children and helps to set the children up for healthy relationships in adulthood.

Childhood experiences shape how we think, act, and build relationships with others in adulthood. Without the proper intervention, these experiences can hinder our growth and development, hold us back in our careers, or lead us down darker paths.

Supporting your children's emotional disposition is an ongoing process that requires attention, patience, and dedication. By identifying their emotional needs, providing consistent support, and encouraging healthy coping mechanisms, you can help your children thrive despite the challenges they face.

Establishing a safe and supportive environment is a continuous process that requires dedication and awareness. By focusing on creating physical and emotional safety, building trust, and maintaining open communication, you can provide a nurturing space for your children to heal and thrive. The road will be bumpy along the way, but the effort will significantly benefit your children.

2

THE HEALING JOURNEY

Healing from emotional abuse is a deeply personal and difficult journey. Before healing can begin, you have to set the intention to begin the healing process. You have to be willing to put in the work and the effort to focus on your personal goals, overcome obstacles, and begin rebuilding what was torn down and broken by your abuser.

There is no right or wrong way to heal. Everyone's journey is unique, and we all take different approaches. What may work for one person may not work for another. This doesn't mean there is something wrong with us; it just means we need a different approach.

This chapter sets the stage for your healing process, emphasizing the importance of self-compassion, patience, and indomitability.

Understanding the Healing Process

Healing from emotional abuse is not easy. It involves ups and downs, small bits of progress, and setbacks. Recognizing this early on in the process can help you be more patient and compassionate with yourself. My stages of healing were acceptance, emotional processing, commitment, and rebuilding.

As you move through the stages of healing, move at your own pace. Recognizing and accepting that you have been abused is the first stage. It is also the stage that takes the longest to get to. Family and friends may notice your situation before you do due to your cognitive dissonance, normalizing the abuse, or wanting to believe your abuser has your best interest at heart.

Once you recognize and accept that you have been emotionally abused, you will begin to process what you have been through and all of the signs of abuse you missed and overlooked. One thing to remember during this time is that it was not your fault that you were abused. No one deserves inhumane treatment. As you move through your emotional processing and consciously decide to begin the healing process, you will shift into the rebuilding and growth stage. Treat yourself with self-compassion and give yourself grace as you move through the process.

You are not a failure, and there is nothing wrong with you. If you can't get out of bed one day because you can't stop crying, let your body release the pain. It's important to let yourself feel the emotions you may have suppressed while living in survival mode. Treat yourself with the same kindness and understanding that you would offer a friend. Recognize your struggles without judgment and allow yourself support and care.

There will be times when you will need to lean on someone. This is where your support systems become important. Family, friends, support groups, and a trauma therapist can help you through all stages of healing. Don't let your pride get in the way of asking for help. You cannot bear the weight of everything on your shoulders, no matter how strong you are. Surround yourself with people who are empathetic, understanding, and supportive. Talking about your experiences with people you trust and feel comfortable with can aid in emotional processing.

> *Reflect on your current support network. Who are the key people you rely on? How often do you reach out to your support network? What apprehensions might prevent you from doing so?*

Tools and Techniques for Healing

As we move through this book, we will discuss various techniques and practices to assist with rebuilding your mind and body.

Mindfulness techniques like meditation and affirmations help calm the mind and reduce stress. There are various forms of guided and unguided meditation to choose from. Technology has made meditation options more abundant, with apps and sessions you can do on your phone.

Body movement to release trauma trapped in the body: Engaging in daily walks, exercise classes, swimming, or other forms of physical activity you enjoy can help release trauma from the body. There is no one "right" way to do this. The key is to incorporate what works for you.

Journaling for emotional release can be a therapeutic way to process your thoughts and feelings. Writing allows you to express emotions that might be difficult to articulate otherwise. Keep a journal handy and ask yourself:

- What emotions am I feeling right now?
- What are my biggest fears?
- How can I address my emotions and biggest fears?

Therapeutic journaling helped me release years of trapped thoughts and emotions that I was unable to express during my sixteen years of marriage.

Creative outlets can also be therapeutic. Activities like drawing, painting, playing music, or crafting can provide a way to express emotions and find joy. Different mental health organizations offer art and music therapy.

Setting Realistic Goals

Set realistic and achievable goals for yourself to focus and motivate you during your journey. Goals help you stay focused, stay on track, and measure your progress along the way. When setting goals, start small. Keep your goals simple and reasonable.

Embracing Growth and Change

Viewing change as a positive force can be empowering. It allows you to see challenges as opportunities for growth and development. By adopting a growth mindset and seeing yourself in a positive light, you will build grit and begin to rebuild your self-esteem and self-worth.

As you progress in your journey, it's important to celebrate your progress, no matter how small, for continued motivation. Acknowledge your achievements and give yourself credit for all of the hard work you've done. Treat yourself to something special, like buying something you have been wanting to purchase, share your success with loved ones, or reflect on your progress in a journal.

Taking the steps to restore mental and physical balance is important for future growth and happiness. It is a journey that requires patience and compassion to overcome the obstacles along the way. Move at your own pace and celebrate your small wins. The journey is a continuous process where each step forward is a step closer to becoming your best self and enjoying life.

3

POSITIVE SELF-PERCEPTION

O nce you make the decision to start on the road of recovery from the mental destruction of emotional abuse, the journey to rebuilding yourself and your self-esteem can begin. Staying focused and determined will assist with seeing positive change within your mind and body. Having a positive self-perception will foster mental endurance and adaptability. The road will be difficult but rewarding.

My biggest success story as a divorce and child custody consultant involved a mother of three in the middle of a divorce and child custody battle with an emotionally abusive husband. When we first met, the mother was just coming to realize that she had been in an abusive relationship. Like me, she remembered her spouse as the man she dated ... loving, charismatic, and caring. However, the man she married and later separated from was hateful, demeaning, insulting, and harsh. In our first conversation, she was brought to tears while telling me what she had endured. I informed her that I could support her on her journey. I also let her know that, with an open mind and a willingness to learn, we could get her strong enough for the mental and physical stress she was about to endure through the family court process.

The mother listened, learned, and followed everything I guided her to do, including self-care and therapy. Her ex began a smear campaign against her to her family, her friends, and their pastor. He escalated his emotional abuse of the children during his custodial visits, leading to one of the children calling the police during an incident. He wanted to reverse everything he agreed to in their signed separation agreement; on top of everything, she lost her job. Her journey was an uphill battle, and it was hard. Not only did she succeed in getting what she wanted in her divorce and child custody battle, but she also represented herself in court during the process.

I followed up with her two years after our first encounter; she was a completely different woman. She was confident, gainfully employed, and engaged! She was happy and successful. Her kids were also doing well. She still has co-parenting struggles, as we all do when leaving abusive relationships, but the tools she learned, such as limited communication, setting healthy boundaries, attending therapy, and self-care, have strengthened her ability to cope.

By shifting her self-perception from a negative focus to a positive focus, she was able to build her confidence and begin the healing and rebuilding process while going through one of the most stressful times of her life. Words cannot express how proud I am of this mother and how honored I am to be a part of her journey.

A positive self-perception assists with rebuilding self-esteem after emotional abuse. Developing a growth mindset, having radical acceptance, and shifting your perspective from negative to positive thinking will help you overcome challenges and thrive in life.

Identifying and Challenging Negative Thoughts

After being chronically emotionally abused over time, we tend to think negatively about ourselves and our abilities. We begin to believe the abuser's insults that are used to manipulate and control us. We may have difficulty making decisions, fear stepping outside our comfort zone and failing, and believe we're not good enough. If emotional abuse begins during childhood, these negative feelings are compounded in adulthood.

What we think, believe, and perceive about ourselves becomes our reality.

"I'm not good at that."
"I could never do that."
"I'm not smart enough."
"I'm a failure."
"I'll never win."

"I'm not attractive."

"I'm fat."

"It's all my fault."

The negative thoughts we generate about ourselves can perpetuate feelings of helplessness and low self-worth.

Write down any recurring negative thoughts you have about yourself. Reflect on how these thoughts impact your daily life and interactions. Now, turn those negative thoughts into positive statements.

Cultivating Positivity

How do you turn those negative thoughts into positive statements? There are many ways we can cultivate positivity in our lives. It can be something as simple as replying, "I'm doing wonderful," when someone asks how you are doing. Even if you are not doing wonderfully at that point and time, you are planting a positive feeling in your mind for your mind to follow.

Additional ways of generating positive feelings in your life include having gratitude, stating affirmations, and visualization exercises. Think about the people you surround yourself with. Are they generally positive people or negative? Do they inspire, uplift, or give positive energy when you are around them? If you consistently feel emotionally drained, have negative feelings, or are imbalanced when you spend time with friends or family, you may want to consider limiting your exposure to them. Surrounding yourself with positive influences, including supportive friends, family, and communities, will positively impact your mood and thoughts.

> *Who are the people in your life that consistently make you feel good about yourself? How can you spend more time with them?*

A simple and easy way to start your day with positive thoughts is to state three things you are grateful for when you wake up. It puts your mind at ease and starts your day off on a positive note. The next step in your morning routine is to look at yourself in the mirror and state three to five positive affirmations about yourself.

Remember those negative statements you turned into positive statements at the beginning of the chapter? Let's start with those and then begin to add additional affirmations. When my children are stressed about an exam or a sporting event coming up, I have them write positive affirmations on sticky notes and place them on the bathroom mirror to read out loud every morning. Here are a few examples of positive affirmations:

"I am worthy of love and respect."
"I am capable of achieving my goals."
"I am successful at everything I focus on."

Another technique for generating positive feelings and energy is visualization. The mind doesn't know the difference between what is real and what is not. When you visualize what you want, the mind begins to work toward that goal to help you achieve it. If you visualize yourself as successful and resilient, your mind will work toward making that vision a reality. Work toward your future self.

These are just a few tips to get you started. There are many ways to begin opening your mind to positive thinking.

Spend a few minutes each day visualizing reaching a specific goal. Notice the feelings and sensations associated with this success. If you can, journal about it.

We all have busy lives, ups and downs, highs and lows. How we choose to handle those situations determines how we feel. Making the conscious choice to be positive can bring you joy and help guide you when faced with difficult decisions. Whenever you feel low or need a helping hand, reach out to your support system.

Consistently practicing positivity is a foundation for rebuilding and healing. Give yourself grace and compassion if you struggle in the beginning with all that life is throwing at you, especially if you've just come out of an emotionally abusive relationship or are having co-parenting difficulties.

Celebrate your small wins. Every little bit helps.

4

HARNESSING THE POWER OF AFFIRMATIONS

I started stating affirmations during my marriage as a coping mechanism for the emotional abuse I was enduring. It was a way for me to incorporate positivity into my life, giving me a boost, even though my ex consistently counteracted them on a daily basis. Affirmations played a significant role in my journey to rebuilding and recovery after I escaped my marriage.

Affirmations are powerful, positive statements and phrases used to uplift and empower mindsets. They are exercises for your mind—a tool for positivity. We state affirmations to ourselves to help achieve goals, improve our mood, and overcome adversity and negative thoughts. Repeating them regularly can reprogram your thinking patterns and influence how you think, act, and feel. Your brain will start to believe in them over time and start making positive changes in your life.

While performing brain studies, Cascio et al.[1] found a significant increase in brain activity in two regions of the brain associated with emotional processing, decision-making, self-perception, and social cognition, concluding that affirmations affect brain activity. They used magnetic resonance imaging (MRI) technology to measure the two parts of the brain following self-affirmation activities.

> *One account of why self-affirmations are successful is attributed to their ability to broaden a person's overall perspective and to reduce the effect of negative emotions.*[2]

Creating Personalized Affirmations

The most effective affirmations are specific to your needs and goals. If you are recovering from an emotionally abusive relationship, constructing affirmations to rebuild self-esteem should be on your list, including affirmations to help you achieve your goals, such as healing. Affirmations should be phrased in the present tense and reflect what you want to achieve.

---

1. Cascio, C. N., et al. (2016). Self-affirmation activates brain systems associated with self-related processing and reward and is reinforced by future orientation. Social Cognitive and Affective Neuroscience, 2016, 621–629.
2. Sherman D.K. (2013). Self-affirmation: understanding the effects. *Social and Personality Psychology Compass*, 7(11), 834–45.

> *What are three areas of your life where you want to see improvement? Create a positive affirmation for each area.*

Integrating Affirmations into Daily Life

Consistency is key when it comes to affirmations. Incorporate them into your daily routine to achieve the best results. It takes thirty days to form a habit. Try stating affirmations for thirty days. At the end of this time, determine what has changed in your life, even if it is something small. Years of emotional abuse can take years to heal. Here are some examples of affirmations that can help boost self-esteem and confidence:

- "I am capable and strong."
- "I deserve all of the good things that happen to me."
- "I believe in myself and my abilities."
- "I am in control of my own happiness."
- "I move through life with confidence."
- "I am capable of accomplishing anything I put my mind to."
- "I love myself unconditionally."
- "I'm a wonderful person."
- "I can prosper and thrive."

Overcoming Resistance to Affirmations

It's common to feel resistance when starting to use affirmations, especially if you've been holding on to negative beliefs for a long time. If your attempts to state them every morning in the mirror are not working, pair them with physical activity, such as deep breathing, exercise, or walking.

You can also write your affirmations on a sticky note every morning to help reinforce the change you are trying to make within your mind. Writing things down triggers brain activity and memory. Also, keep track of your progress to help you stay motivated and to see the impact of your affirmations over time.

> *Start an affirmation journal to track your current affirmations. Write about any shifts in your mindset or behavior that you've noticed since you began stating affirmations.*

Affirmations are a simple yet effective tool for transforming your mindset and building self-esteem and confidence. By creating personalized affirmations and integrating them into your daily life, you can begin to shift your thoughts and beliefs in a positive direction. Just remember, change takes time.

Even though you won't see an immediate change in how you think and feel, don't give up. Trust the process. I've been stating affirmations for years, and I am still a work in progress. I celebrate the small wins and continue to work on rebuilding my self-esteem while restoring my health six years after my marriage separation.

The work of healing continues.

5

THE ROLE OF MEDITATION

Meditation is a prominent practice that can help you heal from emotional abuse by calming the mind, reducing stress, and fostering a deeper connection with yourself. It has been scientifically proven that meditation is a safe and simple way to balance your physical, emotional, and mental state. It has been practiced for thousands of years.

More and more doctors are promoting the practice of meditation to cure many stress-related illnesses. When you slow down your brain rhythm through meditation, your heart rate, metabolism, and breathing rate slow down, which lowers your blood pressure. Endorphins (natural painkillers) are released into your system, giving a sense of calm.

Understanding Meditation

Meditation is not just about sitting still and clearing your mind. Meditation involves focusing the mind and eliminating distractions to achieve a state of relaxation, mental clarity, and calmness.

For survivors of emotional abuse, meditation can be a safe space to process past traumas, release negative energy, and build mental well-being. By focusing on the present moment and practicing mindfulness, you can unravel the layers of pain and self-doubt weighing you down. As survivors, our minds are constantly in overdrive due to hypervigilance. However, we can slow our brains down if we take the time to focus.

I wasn't sleeping because of the stress of possibly losing my children in a child custody dispute; it was starting to have an impact on me physically. However, when my doctor first explained meditation to me and encouraged me to try it as a coping mechanism for the intense stress I was under, I initially refused to listen. It wasn't until she encouraged me to try it for ten minutes every night before bed that I began to see its benefits. I downloaded the meditation app she recommended and did guided meditation for ten minutes before bed for one week. *It was life changing.* I had a good night's sleep every night for the first time in years, waking up refreshed and well-rested. From that week on, I decided to practice meditation every night before bed.

Having an awareness of your thoughts and emotions

helps you to break free from the cycle of manipulation and control imposed through emotional abuse. You can learn to trust your intuition, set healthy boundaries, and reclaim your sense of self-worth. As you practice meditation, you will begin to recognize the patterns of abuse and manipulation in your life, thus developing the heart to break free from their hold on you. I highly recommend including meditation as a part of your daily routine.

Embrace Meditation with an Open Mind

To all survivors of emotional abuse, I invite you to embark on the journey of self-discovery and rebuilding mental toughness through meditation. You are not alone on this journey. You can request a friend to be your accountability partner to help you incorporate meditation into your daily routine, join meditation groups, or simply put meditation on your schedule, setting a reminder to calm your mind and nervous system for a minimum of ten minutes per day.

With each breath and each moment of stillness in meditation, you tap into an abundance of inner power. I encourage you to embrace the practice of meditation with an open heart and an open mind and watch as it leads you toward an empowered future.

Benefits of Meditation for Healing

Regular meditation practice can help reduce anxiety, depression, and stress while improving self-awareness and emotional health. Survivors of emotional abuse often struggle with feelings of worthlessness, anxiety, and low self-esteem. The abuse leaves deep mental scars that take years to heal. The practice of meditation can help with the healing process by calming the nervous system, centering the mind, and helping to develop the inner fight to reclaim a sense of self-worth.

One of the key benefits of meditation is its ability to help you connect with your inner self. It offers survivors of emotional abuse a way to help release trapped emotions and trauma stored in the body. Deep breathing exercises help you focus on your breath and bring awareness to your physical sensations. You begin to release the pain and hurt that have been weighing down your mental and physical body. The emotional release process can be cathartic, allowing you to move forward with a sense of security and freedom.

Mindfulness Meditation Techniques

Deep Breathing Meditation. One beneficial mindfulness technique is deep breathing. By focusing on the breath and bringing awareness to the present moment, survivors can ground themselves in the present, letting go of the pain and hurt of the past. Deep breathing helps survivors release tension and anxiety, promoting a sense of calm and relaxation in both body and mind. Through consistent practice, survivors can learn to use deep breathing as a tool to cope with emotional triggers and moments of distress.

Body Scan Meditation (somatic release). Body scan meditation is a helpful practice for survivors of emotional abuse who struggle with feelings of shame and self-doubt. This practice involves systematically scanning the body from head to toe, focusing on areas of tension, discomfort, or pain. This promotes relaxation and awareness of physical sensations. By tuning into the body's sensations, you can build a deeper connection with yourself while learning to listen to your body's needs. Body scan meditation helps release physical and emotional tension, promoting a sense of relaxation, balance, and self-care.

Visualization Meditation. Visualization is a tool used to create a safe and peaceful inner sanctuary, a place where the mind can retreat in times of stress or overwhelm. By visualizing a place of safety and comfort, survivors can bring about feelings of security. Visualization can help reframe negative thought patterns, induce positive emotions, and envision a future free from the effects of emotional abuse.

Guided Meditation vs. Silent Meditation. Guided meditation involves following along with a recorded voice that leads you through the meditation process, while silent meditation involves sitting quietly and focusing inward. Guided meditation works best for beginners who have difficulty calming themselves when first starting the practice of meditation. When starting the practice, I recommend placing a meditation app on your phone with guided, timed meditations.

> *Try a guided meditation and a silent meditation session. Which one did you find more helpful? Why? How often do you find your mind wandering during the day? How can practicing mindfulness help you stay grounded in the present?*

Integrating Meditation into Your Daily Life

Beginning something new is always a challenge. To begin your meditation journey, start with short, manageable sessions, gradually increasing the duration as you become comfortable. Be patient with yourself as you learn and develop the practice; be persistent in your approach to incorporating the practice into your recovery journey.

Incorporating meditation into your daily life is a healthy coping mechanism for dealing with triggers and emotional challenges that may arise as a result of past abuse, especially if you are co-parenting with your abuser or your abuser was a parent. By learning to ground yourself in the present moment through meditation, you can build a sense of inner security and endurance that will help you navigate difficult emotions and situations with grace and vigor.

Through regular meditation practice, you can build the tools you need to face the lingering effects of emotional abuse head-on, emerging stronger and more resilient than ever before. Find ways to incorporate meditation into your daily routine that will work best for you, such as meditating in the morning, during a break, or before bed. Integrating meditation into your daily life allows you to begin a routine that brings a sense of calm to start and/or end your day.

One of the key benefits of incorporating meditation into your daily routine is the opportunity to create a safe space within yourself. By setting aside time each day for the practice, you can shift your mindset toward a positive one, allowing you to rebuild your self-esteem and confidence.

Remember, healing from emotional abuse is a journey, and it is important to be patient and compassionate with yourself as you make changes to your life. The key is to remain open-minded about the tools and coping mechanisms you may not have considered in the past. By committing to a regular meditation practice, you are taking a step toward reclaiming your inner robustness while finding peace and healing from past traumas. Trust the process, believe in yourself, and know you deserve happiness. Embrace the power of meditation and watch as it helps you find the self-assurance and peace you deserve.

Morning Meditation Routine

Starting your day with a morning meditation routine can set the tone for a positive day. By dedicating just a few minutes each morning to this practice, you can begin your day feeling empowered and ready to take on whatever the day brings.

Evening Meditation for Release and Renewal

In the evening, as the day winds down and the world grows quiet, it is the perfect time to engage in a meditation practice for release and renewal. As survivors of emotional abuse, it is important to take this time for yourself to let go of the pain and negativity that may still linger within you. By engaging in this evening meditation, you are giving yourself the gift of healing and self-care.

Begin by finding a quiet and comfortable space to sit or lie down without distractions. Close your eyes and take a few deep breaths, allowing yourself to relax and let go of any tension in your body. As you continue to breathe deeply, imagine releasing all of the negative emotions and thoughts that have been weighing you down throughout the day.

Focus on the present moment; let go of any worries about the future or regrets about the past. Allow yourself to simply be in this moment, fully present and aware of your thoughts and feelings. As you practice mindfulness this way, you will begin to feel a sense of peace and calm wash over you, releasing any pent-up emotions (see my note earlier) and allowing renewal to occur within you.

Visualize a bright light surrounding you, filling you with compassion and positive energy. Feel this light cleansing you of any residual pain or trauma from your past experiences. Allow yourself to bask in this light and feel its warmth and comfort wrapping around you like a protective cocoon.

As you conclude your evening meditation, take a moment to express gratitude for the tenacity that lies within you. You have survived emotional abuse, having come out stronger on the other side.

Meditation and Other Practices

Meditation is a valuable tool for strengthening the mind and self-discovery. Incorporating it into your daily life can cultivate peace, durability, and emotional safety. You can also combine meditation with other practices, such as yoga, journaling, or affirmations, to enhance its benefits, creating a more comprehensive mental recovery routine.

Remember, self-discovery and growth are not linear processes but rather a series of peaks and valleys leading to greater self-awareness. Trust in the impact of meditation to guide you toward healing, knowing you have the power within to overcome the effects of emotional abuse. Embrace this journey with bravery and determination, knowing that the light at the end of the tunnel is within reach.

You are a survivor, a warrior, and a beacon of hope for

others on their path to restoration. Keep shining bright, and never forget the inner fierceness that resides within you. Celebrate your wins—no matter how small—along the way.

Final Thoughts

Meditation is a valuable tool for survivors of emotional abuse. As survivors begin to practice meditation, they may notice a shift in their mindset. They may begin to feel more grounded, centered, and empowered. By incorporating practices such as deep breathing, body scan meditation, and visualization into daily routines, survivors can release suppressed emotions, boost self-esteem and confidence, and develop toughness in the face of emotional trauma.

Through consistent practice and dedication, survivors can learn to harness meditation to heal from the wounds of the past, embracing a future filled with hope, self-love, and empowerment.

Write down three specific benefits you hope to gain from meditating. How will these benefits support your healing journey?

6

HEALING THROUGH BODY MOVEMENT

Once upon a time, the trend in psychology was "talk about it, and you'll feel better." Over time and through years of research, psychologists have discovered that just talking about how bad we feel keeps us stuck in that feeling. To feel better, we must do something actionable besides talking about our negative feelings.

My daughter and I have a conversation at least every few months about her recovery progress. At one time, she was not fully committed to taking the necessary steps to begin recovery and feel better; her norm was living in her trauma. She was comfortable in that space, and any efforts to create a sense of calm were rejected. Calmness was foreign to her and made her feel *uncomfortable*. Therefore, her trauma recovery journey has been difficult, with periods of regression.

Since my daughter's healing journey is her own, and what she feels comfortable with doing to progress, I support her the best I can as the "safe" person in her life that she knows will protect her at all costs.

Understanding Trauma

Trauma lives in the body. Cortisol, the stress hormone, is released during trauma, as well as during the recollection of trauma. When released during cycles of emotional abuse without a physical outlet, it is trapped within the body, often leading to PTSD. The human brain rewires in survivors of abuse as a response to trauma. It is the brain's way of protecting itself.

Experiencing multiple traumas impacts the body and mind over time. Certain parts of the brain become sensitive, keeping the brain on high alert to perceived threats, which can make victims jumpy and anxious. The part of the brain associated with memory can actually shrink, making it difficult to form new memories. Repetitive stress affects mood, leads to anxiety disorders, and can lead to chronic pain. The energy of trauma lives in body tissue (primarily muscles and fascia) until it can be released through energy-releasing techniques, such as Tai Chi. Stored trauma typically leads to chronic pain, progressively degrading health.

Clinical Therapies for Trauma

Therapies that connect the mind and body can help survivors treat trauma held in the body. Some examples include Cognitive Processing Therapy (CPT), Prolonged Exposure (PE) Therapy, and Eye Movement Desensitization and Reprocessing (EMDR) therapy.

I personally participated in EMDR therapy for six months; it was the best decision of my life. It helped my brain process traumatic events differently. Certain smells and words still trigger me; however, my body does not respond with sweaty palms, increased heart rate, and bodily shakes like it used to. I'm able to continue functioning after experiencing a trigger; my trigger responses have significantly declined over time.

Body Movement Therapy

As survivors of emotional abuse, trauma is a heavy burden that many of us carry. The pain and suffering can feel unbearable at times, but there is hope through the use of body movement practices.[1]

---

1. Sornborger J, Fann A, Serpa JG, Ventrelle J, R D N MS, Ming Foynes M, Carleton M, Sherrill AM, Kao LK, Jakubovic R, Bui E, Normand P, Sylvia LG. Integrative Therapy Approaches for Posttraumatic Stress Disorder: A Special Focus on Treating Veterans. Focus (Am Psychiatr Publ). 2017 Oct;15(4):390-398. doi: 10.1176/appi.focus.20170026. Epub 2017 Oct 12. PMID: 31975869; PMCID: PMC6519541.

Dance Therapy. Not only is dancing fun, but through dance movement, survivors can experience a physical release of tension through creative expression. Dance therapy allows survivors of emotional abuse to express themselves through movement, releasing emotions stored in the body that may be difficult to put into words. By moving your body in a safe and supportive environment, you can release the trauma stored in your muscles and tissues. Dance therapy also helps you reconnect with your body in a positive way, building self-confidence and self-esteem.

Yoga. Yoga[2] is another practice that can aid in healing from emotional abuse. Through a series of poses and breathing exercises, you can release tension and stress stored in your body. The combination of breathwork, mindfulness, and physical postures can help survivors reconnect with their bodies and minds. By tuning into the present moment through yoga, survivors can learn to let go of past hurts and develop a sense of peace.

I am a huge fan of yoga. However, I wasn't always. When I first started the practice, I didn't like the slow, purposeful movements. It wasn't until I saw the benefits of flexibility,

---

2. English A, McKibben E, Sivaramakrishnan D, Hart N, Richards J, Kelly P. A Rapid Review Exploring the Role of Yoga in Healing Psychological Trauma. Int J Environ Res Public Health. 2022 Dec 3;19(23):16180. doi: 10.3390/ijerph192316180. PMID: 36498254; PMCID: PMC9741324.

tension release, and mind-calming that I fell in love with the practice.

In addition to its physical and emotional benefits, yoga offers a sense of community and support for survivors. By attending classes or workshops with others, individuals can connect with like-minded individuals who understand their experiences and offer encouragement and solidarity. Yoga studios and teachers often create a safe and nurturing environment for survivors to explore their healing process, providing a sense of belonging and acceptance.

As you embark on your healing journey through yoga, remember to approach the practice with an open heart and mind, allowing yourself to be present and compassionate with yourself. Trust in the process, knowing that each breath and movement on the mat is a step toward reclaiming your power and finding freedom from the effects of emotional abuse.

Embrace the practice of yoga as a tool for self-discovery and self-love. Embrace it, knowing that you have the persistence and perseverance within you to overcome past traumas.

Tai Chi. Tai Chi. This ancient Chinese martial art is a physical exercise and meditative practice that focuses on the mind-body connection. The slow, deliberate movements of Tai Chi promote relaxation and focus, allowing survivors to release tension and stress. Through Tai Chi, survivors can learn to ground themselves in the present moment, letting go of the pain of the past. Tai Chi can provide a much-needed sense of calm and peace.

I practiced Tai Chi while quarantined during the COVID-19 pandemic, and my younger son participated as well. It was a way for us to bond as mother and son and provided mental and physical activity during a difficult time.

Incorporating Tai Chi into a healing routine can help survivors of emotional abuse regain a sense of control over their bodies and minds. By embracing the calming effects of Tai Chi, survivors can begin to rebuild their sense of self-worth and self-esteem.

Walking and Nature Therapy

Walking, especially in nature, can be a soothing and accessible form of exercise. It helps us clear our brains and release tension. It's a simple exercise we can incorporate into our daily routines. Taking a simple walk during a work break or after work can do wonders for our minds and bodies. Walking in nature offers an ideal place to help heal our pains and provides a visual sense of calm.

According to the American Physiological Association, there is an 18% lower risk of depression among adults who get half of the recommended amount of physical activity per week compared with adults who report no physical activity. A study comparing outdoor walking during psychotherapy outpatient trauma therapy sessions with sedentary behavior concluded, "*Integrating walking into psychotherapy is a novel opportunity to improve cardiovascular risk factors and symptoms of mental illness, support emotion regulation, facilitate therapeutic alliance and integration of therapy skills, and habitualize walking.*"[3]

The Connection Between Body and Mind

It is important to understand how physical activity influences mental balance and helps in the healing process. The mind and body are intricately connected, and by tuning into your body through movement, you can begin to release the repressed emotions that have been weighing you down. Dance therapy, yoga, Tai Chi, and mindful movement practices are all effective ways to connect with your body.

Incorporating Movement into Daily Life

Developing a routine that fits your lifestyle and preferences is key to maintaining consistency and reaping the benefits of physical activity for processing trauma. Find opportunities

---

3. Whitworth JW, Craft LL, Dunsiger SI, Ciccolo JT. Direct and indirect effects of exercise on posttraumatic stress disorder symptoms: a longitudinal study. *Gen Hosp Psychiatry*. 2017;49:56-62.

for movement throughout the day to stay active. You can incorporate movement into daily activities, such as taking the stairs instead of the elevator, stretching during breaks, walking during lunch, or having a dance break while cooking. Where there is a will, there's a way.

I found it easiest to add yoga to my morning routine. Before beginning my day, I do fifteen minutes of yoga to prepare myself mentally and physically for the day. I've found that whenever I feel tension or pressure in my muscles due to stress, regular yoga practices help to relieve it.

> *Identify three ways you can add*
> *more movement to your daily routine.*

Overcoming Barriers to Physical Activity

Common barriers to maintaining a regular exercise routine can slow us down and impact our healing journey. Barriers, such as time constraints, lack of motivation, or physical limitations, impact our path. Set a weekly plan of physical activity for yourself to help keep you on track, making sure it is feasible and is something you can follow and commit to.

Add enjoyable activities to your plan. Don't pick doing Tai Chi four days a week if it is not something you enjoy. Select a body movement activity you enjoy and commit to the plan. Finding an accountability partner or body movement partner will also help you stay on track.

Physical movement assists with removing trauma from

the body. Incorporating regular physical activity into your life can enhance your physical and emotional fitness. Every bit of movement counts. Don't get discouraged when you fall off the wagon one week due to emergencies or last-minute events. Get back on track next week and give yourself grace. Celebrate the small wins.

Moving your body can help with trapped emotions in the body, release stress, and build endurance. By tuning into your body and listening, you can begin to heal from the wounds of emotional abuse and start to feel empowered.

7

TAKING ACTION TOWARD EMPOWERMENT

Taking action toward empowerment is a step toward reclaiming your identity and moving forward after emotional abuse. You've been through a lot; now, it is time to take back the power you lost to feel whole again. Becoming empowered involves setting achievable goals, making decisions, and taking the necessary steps toward creating the life you want.

Change is difficult for everyone; when you are trying to heal from emotional trauma and rebuild your self-esteem, it makes the journey more difficult. It's a process. Every step, no matter how small, is significant. By making a plan and taking small, consistent actions, you can achieve your goals on the road to long-term empowerment. The challenge you face is having faith in yourself and trusting the process.

Setting Realistic and Achievable Goals

Goal setting is a great resource for creating direction and purpose. It helps focus your energy to take concrete steps toward your desired outcomes. By establishing goals, you are setting the mental intention to achieve them.

S-M-A-R-T goals are:

1. Specific
2. Measurable
3. Achievable
4. Relevant, and
5. Time-bound.

When you establish S-M-A-R-T goals, you are not only setting your goals but also making a plan and timeline to achieve them. We typically set S-M-A-R-T goals in our work environments to measure success; however, you can use the same tool in your personal life as a guide to achieving personal development goals. As you think about goal setting, think about the areas in your life where you wish to improve.

Some categories may be:

- Sleep goals for quality rest and mood regulation
- Social engagement activities to reduce feelings of loneliness and isolation
- Therapy and stress management goals to assist with the emotional abuse healing process

Here are a few examples to get you started:

- "I will meditate for ten minutes every day for the next month."
- "I will walk for thirty minutes, four times a week, for the next eight weeks."
- "I will journal for ten minutes every evening for the next thirty days."
- "I will spend thirty minutes, twice a week, engaging in a hobby I enjoy for the next three weeks."

Tips For Setting S-M-A-R-T Empowerment Goals

Think about what's important to you and what you want to achieve.

Identify your values. Setting goals that align with your values will help you stay motivated and focused to achieve them.

Start with small, achievable goals. Don't try to boil the ocean! If you have a larger goal in mind, break it into smaller, achievable steps. Small wins help you build confidence. It also helps you get past the feelings of perfectionism and fear of failure.

Be clear on what you want to achieve. Be as specific and detailed as possible to help you stay focused and on track. Without a clear goal, you won't have a clear path, and you won't achieve your outcome.

Be flexible. Things are not always going to go as planned, no matter how well thought-out your goals are. Life happens. You can adjust your goals as needed. Please be kind to yourself when setbacks or challenges occur.

Celebrate small wins. Celebrating small wins along your journey can help keep you motivated to build momentum. Psychologically, we are more likely to achieve goals and stay consistent when we reward ourselves for our wins. Treat yourself to something you enjoy.

Find an accountability partner. Setting and achieving goals is a challenging process. By having an accountability partner in place, they can help you stay on track and motivated. An accountability partner can be family, friends, a therapist, a coach, or a support group.

Build a support network. Surround yourself with supportive and encouraging people. A strong support network provides motivation, accountability, and emotional support.

Maintain motivation and momentum. Staying motivated and maintaining momentum are both difficult and needed for long-term success. Burnout, distractions, and unexpected events can derail us. What keeps me on track and focused is my desire to heal and be empowered. I never want anyone to have the control over me that I experienced in my marriage.

Establishing regular check-ins with your accountability partner, rewarding yourself for progress, no matter how small, and staying connected to your support network will help you succeed.

> *What three specific goals do you want to achieve in the next six months?*

Identifying barriers to achieving S-M-A-R-T Goals

While developing your S-M-A-R-T goals, consider potential barriers to achieving each goal. For example, if I set a goal of waking up at 7:00 a.m. every morning, there may be a barrier to having a good night's sleep, preventing me from being motivated to get up. I need a barrier-removal plan to ensure I

DR. ALANA SHARPS

meet my goal and set myself up for success. I could set my alarm clock in a place that forces me to get up. I could also plan something enjoyable after waking up, such as grabbing morning tea or looking forward to my new yoga session with my community.

Think of barriers that may impact your ability to meet your identified goals and discover different ways of setting yourself up for success. Be creative in how you might navigate challenges that arise in achieving your goals.

Taking Risks and Embracing Change

Taking risks and embracing change are necessary for growth. Stepping out of your comfort zone can lead to new opportunities and personal development. As you develop your S-M-A-R-T goals, identify stretch goals along the way. Maybe you have always thought about taking a suspension exercise class, but were too afraid to try it. Try it out! Try new things and see what you like. Open your horizons. There is no one holding you back!

The Ongoing Process of Goal Setting

Goal setting is an ongoing process. As you achieve your goals, set new ones and keep repeating this process. Setting goals requires patience, perseverance, and flexibility. By taking the time to set goals that align with your values and priorities while identifying an accountability partner (family, friend, or coach), you can make progress and achieve your goals over time. As always, give yourself grace; focus on how your goals will help improve your life and happiness.

While setting goals is important, it's also important to prioritize self-care. Listen to your mind and body; give yourself permission to rest as needed. Remember to be patient with yourself and compassionate as you execute your action plan. Every step forward is significant and worth celebrating.

Taking action toward empowerment is a journey that requires commitment, stamina, and support. By setting goals, overcoming obstacles, and celebrating progress, you can reclaim who you are and create a life that reflects your true self.

8

BUILDING HEALTHY RELATIONSHIPS

Healthy relationships are essential for emotional prosperity and personal growth. After experiencing emotional abuse, it is crucial that one learn how to build and maintain relationships that are supportive, respectful, and nurturing.

Setting boundaries is a key component of staying mentally sound and maintaining positive, healthy relationships. They are the limits of appropriate behavior between people and affect intimate relationships, families, and colleagues in a work environment. This can be challenging and often uncomfortable, but it ensures how we interact with one another and provides emotional safety.

∼

Characteristics of Healthy Intimate Partner Relationships

Healthy, intimate partner relationships are built on mutual respect, trust, and open communication. They involve a balance of give and take, allowing both individuals to grow. Key characteristics of a healthy intimate partner relationship are:

- Your partner is respectful and values your opinions, feelings, and needs.
- You can talk openly to your partner and feel heard.
- You enjoy spending time apart, alone, or with others.
- You trust your partner, and your partner trusts you.
- You are equal in the relationship. One person does not have control over the other.
- You have emotional as well as physical intimacy.
- You address conflict with your partner without judgment or contempt and can often find a compromise or solution.

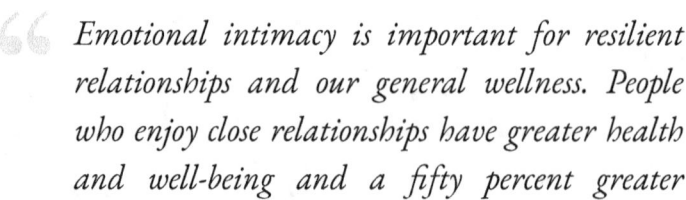 *Emotional intimacy is important for resilient relationships and our general wellness. People who enjoy close relationships have greater health and well-being and a fifty percent greater*

likelihood of living a longer life (Holt-Lunstad, 2010) than those who don't.[1] *And research consistently finds that "people are most likely to thrive when they feel intimately connected to significant others (Pietromonoco, 2017).*[2]

Recognizing Toxic Relationships and Patterns

Recognizing and understanding the signs of toxic relationships is important in order to avoid them. Your relationships should contribute to a sense of fulfillment, happiness, and connection. If you tend to feel more anxious, distressed, or unhappy around your partner, your relationship may be unhealthy.

For example, during my marriage, I dreaded Fridays because I knew I had to spend the weekend with my husband, walking on eggshells, trying to navigate his mood swings. My marriage was a toxic relationship. These are signs of a possible toxic relationship:

- Disagreements or discussions go through a "word salad" and go nowhere.

1. Holt-Lunstad J, Smith TB, Layton JB (2010) Social Relationships and Mortality Risk: A Meta-analytic Review. PLOS Medicine 7(7): e1000316. https://doi.org/10.1371/journal.pmed.1000316
2. Pietromonaco, P. R., & Collins, N. L. (2017). Interpersonal mechanisms linking close relationships to health. The American psychologist, 72(6), 531–542. https://doi.org/10.1037/amp0000129

- You don't feel happy or comfortable around your partner.
- You're afraid of expressing disagreement.
- You walk on eggshells to keep the peace.
- You don't feel heard or seen in the relationship when you express your feelings.
- Your partner says negative or hurtful things to you.
- The relationship feels unequal in power.
- Your partner ignores your boundaries.

If you feel any of the above in your relationship, you may be in a toxic relationship. Take a serious look at your relationship and evaluate your situation. Toxic relationships erode self-esteem and self-worth.

Setting Boundaries and Asserting Yourself

Healthy boundaries define what is appropriate behavior in our relationships — behavior that keeps both parties safe. Establishing and maintaining boundaries protects your emotional health and sets the stage for positive relationships.

Setting healthy boundaries requires self-awareness. You need to be clear on your expectations for yourself and for others, as well as what you are and are not comfortable with in different situations. You also need to clearly communicate your boundaries to others. This does not mean making demands. It simply means clearly articulating in a way that requires people to listen to you.

Here are three simple ways to establish healthy boundaries:

1. Speak clearly and be as straightforward as possible without raising your voice.
2. State your request in terms of what you want, not what you don't want.
3. Accept the discomfort that comes as a result of expressing your boundaries. You may feel guilt, shame, or remorse, and that's okay.

Some adults were taught in childhood that expressing their needs is a bad thing and makes them selfish. However, healthy boundaries are required for your emotional and mental health, autonomy, and identity.

Below are a few examples of healthy boundaries:

- Declining anything you don't want to do.
- Truly expressing your feelings.
- Transparently talking about your experiences. No sugarcoating.
- Replying in the moment instead of regretting not replying later.
- Addressing problems directly with the person involved.
- Making your expectations clear.

When we don't establish firm boundaries, we allow others to walk all over us, settling for unhealthy relationships that lead to resentment, manipulation, and abuse. Research has shown that in families with healthy boundaries, everyone can develop their identity with unique interests and skills while also having a sense of individuality, self-worth, and self-esteem. When people do not have the chance to learn how to set healthy boundaries in childhood, it can lead to challenges for them as adults.

People who have been abused as children may not know healthy boundaries; they enter into intimate partner relationships with abusive partners because the treatment is familiar and comfortable. Abused children often grow up with a lack of control over their emotional and physical boundaries.

Fostering Healthy and Supportive Relationships

It's important to surround yourself with positive influences and seek relationships that add value to your life. Building healthy relationships involves nurturing connections with people who support and uplift you. If the people you surround yourself with consistently make you feel uncomfortable, uneasy, or not at peace, you may need to re-evaluate your relationship with them.

> *Identify three people in your life who*
> *consistently support and encourage you.*

Effective Communication Skills

Open and honest communication is the foundation of any healthy relationship. Being transparent about mutual needs and expectations leads to healthy, intimate partnerships and involves clearly expressing your thoughts and feelings while actively listening to others. Remember to listen to understand, not to respond.

Practice asserting yourself by role-playing with a friend, coach, or therapist.

- "I'm not comfortable with this."
- "Please do not..."
- "This doesn't work for me."
- "I've decided not to..."
- "I'm drawing the line at..."
- "I don't want to do that."

A healthy relationship with yourself is the foundation for healthy relationships with others. Building healthy relationships is a vital part of your healing journey. By recognizing toxic patterns, setting boundaries, fostering positive connections, and cultivating self-love, you can create relationships that support you rather than tear you down.

Building healthy relationships with all people in your life takes time and effort and is also a learning process, especially if you are an adult who has lived without having any boundaries in your relationships, dating back to childhood.

Boundaries protect our physical and mental space, like fences that give privacy and help neighbors feel safe. Boundaries are the physical and emotional limits of appropriate behavior between people. They help define where one person ends and another begins.

9

_____

SELF-CARE AND SELF-COMPASSION

Self-care and self-compassion involve taking deliberate actions to care for your physical, emotional, and mental fitness—different aspects of treating yourself with kindness and understanding. Think of self-care as *treating* yourself kindly and self-compassion as *considering* yourself kindly. It's the difference between doing and being, acting and thinking. It's a distinction that we need to make in order to get meaningful results from our self-care and view ourselves in a positive light.

Understanding Self-Care

Self-care is not the same as being "selfish." It is the practice of taking care of your mental and physical health. It's prioritizing your needs and making time for yourself. It encompasses activities and practices that help you maintain your health, including physical care, emotional care, mental care, and social care. When you prioritize your physical, emotional, and social needs, you'll experience less stress and anxiety, better sleep, increased energy, and enhanced mood.

Physical Self-Care Activities:

- Read instead of scrolling through your phone before bed.
- Try a new healthy recipe.
- Replace your nightcap with herbal tea.
- Get a massage.
- Go to bed earlier.

Emotional Self-Care Activities:

- Journaling.
- Therapy.
- Taking breaks and relaxing.
- Engaging in activities that bring joy and fulfillment.
- Reducing and managing stress.

Social Self-Care Activities:

- Socializing with friends and family.
- Going out and meeting new people.
- Keeping in touch with old friends.

- Volunteering with an organization.
- Going to community events.

> *What self-care activities do you currently engage in?*

Creating a Self-Care Routine

Practicing self-care is difficult when you've always prioritized others over yourself. Developing a regular self-care routine ensures that you consistently take time to nurture yourself by addressing your mental and physical needs. You start by prioritizing your needs, setting a goal, and making a plan.

Think about what you enjoy doing and what relaxes you as a starting point for your self-care plan. Maybe walking or getting a massage is your thing. Whatever works best for you. Pull out your calendar and pick dates and times; commit to those activities during the week. If you don't write it down and schedule it, it won't happen. Be realistic with your activities and goals. If something doesn't work or go according to plan, that's okay. Reassess and redo the plan. This is for you, not anyone else.

Understanding Self-Compassion

Self-compassion is treating yourself with understanding, acceptance, and kindness. It involves treating yourself with the same kindness and understanding that you would offer a friend. It means acknowledging your struggles without judgment and offering yourself support and care. We tend to give everything of ourselves to others, but don't provide ourselves with the same compassion. We are all our worst critics and our worst enemies.

When you've been emotionally abused for years, you start to believe the words of your abuser and internalize them. Their words become your worst critic. Self-compassion is our armor against our negative thoughts and is one of the most valuable tools we can possess.

> *How do you typically respond to your own mistakes or failures? How can you practice more self-compassion in these situations?*

Practicing Self-Compassion

Self-compassion can be practiced through techniques such as self-soothing, positive self-talk, and compassionate writing. You can practice mindfulness techniques such as meditation to calm your mind and affirmations to build your self-esteem and worthiness. You can also choose to write a letter to yourself. I wrote myself a letter of forgiveness for staying in my marriage for as long as I did and not recognizing the harm it was doing to my children. The guilt and shame I felt for impacting their mental and physical safety were hard to bear at times, affecting my day-to-day life.

Writing a letter to yourself is a helpful way of expressing self-acceptance, understanding, and compassion.

It provides acknowledgment and understanding with a compassionate perspective to help influence the way we think about a situation. Write your letter from the perspective of someone who cares about you, understands you, and accepts you for who you are. Imagine the person is supportive, understanding, accepting, kind, and forgiving.

As you think about your experience, write what your friend might say to you regarding how you feel about yourself and your experiences. Below are some suggestions for writing your compassionate letter to yourself:

- Acknowledge how you are feeling and that it is okay to feel this way.
- Remind yourself that you are human; everyone makes mistakes.
- Write what your forgiving friend might offer as a way to look at things differently.
- Add any suggestions that the forgiving friend might offer to help you feel better, address the problem, and move on from it.
- Think about how your forgiving friend would say these things in a kind, understanding way.

Combining Self-Care and Self-Compassion

Integrating self-care and self-compassion creates a holistic approach to nurturing your body. It ensures that you address your emotional and physical needs as well as your mindset.

> *How can you combine self-care and self-compassion in your routine?*

Overcoming Barriers to Self-Care & Self-Compassion

Common barriers to self-care and self-compassion include time constraints, feelings of guilt, and ingrained negative beliefs. Work and family obligations can make it challenging to prioritize health for self-care. However, we need to make time. One way to integrate self-care into your week is to break up the activities into more manageable tasks.

Do a ten-minute morning workout in your home instead of going to a gym class. It's more convenient and time efficient. If low motivation is a factor due to feeling overwhelmed, low, or stressed during the week, try setting small, achievable goals, such as not eating out for a week. As always, accountability partners are great for keeping you on track, motivating, and supporting you on this journey.

Barriers to self-compassion include constant self-criticism, feeling unworthy or deserving of compassion, and feeling that we deserve to feel shame, guilt, and empty feelings. If self-criticism began in childhood, it is more than likely an integral part of adulthood. However, self-criticism can become unhealthy and lead to feelings that can significantly impact our current and future lives.

The same is true for feelings of unworthiness of being treated with kindness and understanding when we have negative experiences. The feelings can often be traced back to past childhood experiences that influence our lives. Rebuilding our self-esteem and self-worth through affirmations, therapy, and other mindfulness techniques can assist with overcoming these barriers.

Maintaining Consistency and Adjusting as Needed

Consistency is key to reaping the benefits of self-care and self-compassion. However, adjusting your practices as your needs change is also important. You can maintain consistency in your self-care routine by setting reminders on your phone, tracking your progress, and being flexible as emergencies and unexpected events occur.

Self-care and self-compassion should be non-negotiable aspects of our lives. They are essential wellness components and can assist with healing from emotional abuse and trauma. You can foster a healthier, more balanced life by prioritizing and treating yourself with kindness.

We all deserve care and kindness just as much as anyone else. Don't give so much to others that you forget to take care of yourself. Remember, providing yourself with self-care and self-compassion isn't being selfish. It's about prioritizing and taking care of you.

You will face barriers as you begin to prioritize self-care and self-compassion in your life, and that is okay. It's how we learn to be flexible, realistic, and consistent. When you feel overwhelmed, reach out to friends, family, a therapist, or a coach for support. Remember, small changes go a long way, so take baby steps in the beginning. I believe in you.

Challenge yourself to set a self-care goal this week. You have got this!

10

SUSTAINING AND GROWING YOUR SELF-ESTEEM

Growing and sustaining your self-esteem is an ongoing process that requires continuous effort and self-reflection. It involves building on the foundation you've created thus far and finding ways to maintain and enhance your sense of self-worth over time. It is a journey rather than a destination, which takes time to build.

A positive mindset is also important to embrace along the way. Embracing a positive mindset focused on growth is a continuous process that evolves with experiences and personal development. You will hit roadblocks along your journey as unexpected life experiences come into play. Instead of dwelling on the negative side of emotions, stay focused on the positive. Celebrate your achievements and make practicing gratitude a part of your everyday life.

Building Resilience

Resilience is the ability to bounce back from setbacks and continue moving forward. Building resilience is essential for sustaining self-esteem, especially when facing challenges.

When we have purpose in life, it helps us build resilience. Take the opportunity to discover what interests you. Having experienced trauma and hardship changes your perspective on things. You will become stronger over time as you heal and progress. What you experience will become a learning experience for you. As you move into new relationships with others, you will be more self-aware and feel a greater sense of strength. A greater sense of strength can increase your self-worth and self-esteem.

Consider volunteering at your local homeless shelter, dog shelter, or other organization of interest to you. Not only does this get you out of the house, but it also provides a service to those in need within your community. Volunteering and connecting with others give you purpose, foster self-worth, and empower you as you build resilience.

Be proactive with your life and healing. To become empowered and build resilience, you need to step outside of your comfort zone and rebuild yourself mentally. Acknowledge and accept your emotions during difficult times while developing a plan to tackle your problems to get to the other side. Taking the initiative enables you to build motivation and purpose even during the most stressful periods, increasing the likelihood that you'll rise up during the most painful times of your life again.

Embrace Positivity

Our thoughts become our actions, which impact our futures. When we have experienced trauma, we become hypervigilant. Hypervigilance, meant to protect us from harm, can sometimes cause us to have irrational thinking patterns, making small things into large, catastrophic events. By embracing positivity and positive thinking, we can offset our negative patterns and adopt a more balanced and realistic one.

You will continue to encounter challenges in your life. However, how you interpret and respond to the challenge will make a difference. Your past does not dictate your future. Also, remember that change is a part of life. Maybe you didn't hit all of your goals in life because of your toxic intimate partner relationship or relationship with your toxic parent. Focus on setting new targets for your goals or developing new goals as you rebuild your future and develop resilience. Once you accept circumstances that cannot be changed, you can focus on circumstances that you can alter.

Always remember to be mindful, remember you're not alone in your struggles, and to practice self-care and compassion.

> *Reflect on a recent setback. How did you handle it, and what did you learn from the experience? How will that inform the next reaction to a setback?*

Continuing Personal Development

Create a personal development plan to build self-esteem and resilience. A good plan considers your long-term goals, focusing on what, how, why, and when. Ask yourself:

- What mindfulness skills will I add to my life (journaling, meditation, mindful movement, gratitude, etc.)?
- How will I add them to my life?
- Why will I add them to my life?
- When will I add them?

A great start is to create a thirty-day action plan. Studies have shown it takes a minimum of thirty days to build a habit and retrain your mind. Once you have completed the first thirty days, develop a new thirty-day plan for continued development.

Personal development involves continuously seeking opportunities to learn and grow. Engaging in new experiences and acquiring new skills can enhance your self-esteem, broaden your horizons, uplift your mood, and strengthen your resilience.

Practicing Gratitude

Gratitude is a tool for maintaining a positive outlook and sustaining self-esteem. Regularly acknowledging and appreciating the good things in your life can enhance your overall happiness. Consider starting a gratitude journal to write down what you are thankful for each day. Shifting your focus to the positive things happening in your life helps to focus and calm your mind from the everyday stress of life.

Monitoring and Adjusting Your Progress

Regularly monitoring your progress and making necessary adjustments helps you stay on track with your self-esteem goals. It allows you to recognize what's working and what needs improvement. Use a journal, checklist, or phone app to monitor your progress and stay on track with your goals. It also helps you to look back on your progress and see how far you have come. You'll be surprised by how much you have developed over time.

Set aside time each week to review your progress. What have you accomplished, and what adjustments do you need to make to stay aligned with your goals?

Professional Help

Sometimes, maintaining and growing self-esteem may require professional support. Therapists and counselors can provide guidance and strategies tailored to your specific needs. Trauma therapists are recommended for healing from trauma. They are trained in trauma therapies to assist with your healing. Asking for help is not a sign of weakness. Don't limit your healing by refusing to ask for help due to pride or societal stigmatism.

Sustaining and growing your self-esteem is a lifelong journey that requires dedication, self-awareness, and continuous effort. By incorporating these practices into your daily life, you can maintain a healthy sense of self-worth and continue to thrive. Create a personal development plan to guide you on your journey and keep you focused. With focus comes dedication and purpose. If you need additional support, therapists and counselors are available to assist with a therapy plan tailored to your specific needs.

As you go along your journey, celebrate your progress and be patient with yourself. It is not a race to heal as fast as you can; it is a slow journey to rebuilding yourself. Self-esteem growth is a gradual process, and every step forward counts.

CONCLUSION
EMBRACING YOUR NEW SELF

As you reach the end of this book, it's time to reflect on your journey, celebrate your progress, and look forward to the future. Embracing your new self involves recognizing the growth you've achieved and continuing to nurture your self-esteem and confidence.

- You are worthy of respect.
- You are important.
- You are valued.

Reflecting on Your Journey

As you embrace your healing journey, it's important to self-reflect and note your achievements. Maybe you are getting more sleep, you're not a nervous wreck every time you see your ex, or you've become more social. All of these things are accomplishments that should be celebrated.

The first two days after leaving my ex-husband, I didn't know what to do with my time. My life centered around him, his wants, and his needs. When my time was finally my own, I was lost. I had to find myself again. What I liked, what I didn't like, and what activities I enjoyed. It took me some time to figure things out, but once I began to push myself into the outside world again, on my terms, I celebrated each achievement along the way.

Taking time to reflect on your progress allows you to appreciate the hard work and dedication you've put into your journey. If you haven't started a journal yet, now is a great time to write about your experiences, noting the challenges you've faced and overcome, as well as the milestones you've achieved. Celebrations bring us joy, enhance our mood, and make us feel good overall.

Recognizing and celebrating your achievements, no matter how small, is important for maintaining motivation to continue to move forward.

Embracing Your New Identity

Embracing your new self involves accepting and loving who you have become. It means recognizing your strengths, acknowledging your growth, and being proud of your journey.

> *What aspects of your new identity*
> *are you most proud of?*

Maintaining Your Growth

Continuing to nurture your self-esteem and confidence is an ongoing process. It involves staying committed to the practices and habits that have supported your growth. Your newfound habits of self-care and mindfulness activities will continue to assist with your mental and physical health as you move through life.

Remember to stay connected to others and continue to set new goals for a new focus and growth. Setting future goals helps you stay focused and motivated. It provides direction and purpose as you continue your journey. The world continuously changes around us. How we adapt to change through continued self-development determines how we will get through life's challenges. Embrace change as an opportunity for learning and development.

Your Journey Ahead

Your journey doesn't end here; it continues as you move forward with the tools and insights you've gained. Embrace your new self with confidence and optimism. Remember to be patient and kind to yourself along the way. You will have hurdles to overcome, and everything will not go as planned. Practice self-compassion and give yourself grace. You will get back on track with determination and the drive to continue the journey.

You are strong, resilient, and capable of achieving great things. Embrace your new self with pride and continue to nurture your self-esteem and confidence. You have the ability to shape your future and live a fulfilling life.

CASE STUDIES

CASE STUDY #1: *Understanding the Impact of an Emotionally Abusive Parent*

Ellen, a 45-year-old divorced mom of three, grew up with an emotionally abusive mother who wanted Ellen to dress in her image, so she controlled what Ellen wore. She consistently teased Ellen about her acne and the unruly nature of her African American hair and criticized everything she did. Not only was she overly critical, but she also didn't display any love or affection, leaving Ellen emotionally neglected.

Ellen grew up believing her mother didn't love her and that there was nothing she could do to please her. Over time, Ellen's self-esteem plummeted, and she became increasingly self-conscious and withdrawn. Her mother's constant criticism, belittling, and gaslighting made Ellen doubt her ability to succeed in anything she attempted to pursue, making her feel her feelings were not warranted. These feelings shaped Ellen's adulthood. It didn't help that her mother continued to demean and tease Ellen in front of family and friends as a means of embarrassment.

The emotional abuse Ellen suffered held her back in many ways. In an effort to receive the love, acceptance, and affection Ellen so desperately wanted from her mother, she chose to do things that were challenging, hoping her mother would be proud of her. However, no matter how successful Ellen became, she still felt like a failure. She became an overachiever, never feeling that her success was attributed to her abilities or competence. She developed imposter syndrome, a negative thinking pattern that prevents people from recognizing their success. This limited her ability to grow in her career. She was afraid to speak up in professional settings for fear of being incorrect and did not apply for promotions, believing she didn't have the skill set to excel and be successful.

Ellen also had difficulty receiving love and compliments. After being criticized her entire life for her appearance, compliments were uncomfortable, as well as unbelievable. No matter how clear the imperfections on Ellen's skin appeared, she still saw problem areas that needed to be addressed.

During her mid-twenties, Ellen met and fell in love with her soulmate, not realizing that her prince charming was a narcissist. The love bombing stage of the emotional abuse cycle made Ellen feel loved and appreciated. Love bombing is a term used to describe emotional manipulation in the early stages of a relationship. Victims often experience immense flattery, gifts, and excessive attention to appeal to their hearts, weaken their defense mechanisms, and allow them to be drawn into a whirlwind romance without even realizing it.

When the emotional abuse began in the relationship, the behavior and treatment Ellen experienced were so familiar to her childhood with her mother that she didn't realize she was being abused.

The emotional abuse Ellen suffered in her marriage took a toll on her mentally and physically over a period of many years until Ellen was able to escape the relationship. It was through therapy that Ellen learned her attraction to the narcissist was from the familiar nature of how she was treated in her childhood by her first bully... her mother.

CASE STUDY #2: The Power of Affirmations and Meditation During High-Conflict Legal Cases

I had a client a few years ago who was being repeatedly dragged through the legal system by her high-powered attorney ex-husband. For the sake of anonymity, we'll call her Agnes. Agnes had a permanent child custody order and a parent coordinator to assist with tie-breaking decisions; however, she still did not have any joint decision-making authority. The parent coordinator allowed her ex-husband to make decisions without consulting with her first, as he refused to follow the order as written and continued to manipulate family court officials into believing my client was crazy. She wasn't crazy; she was traumatized from continuous emotional abuse.

While married, Agnes' ex-husband led her to believe she needed to be admitted to a mental institution for help, to which she obliged. Her ex-husband's continued gaslighting, manipulation, and control kept her second-guessing her thoughts and feelings, leading her to believe she needed to be admitted to the institution. She was released days after admission following a thorough assessment. She never needed to be admitted, but the stigma remained on her record, to be used by her ex-husband against her during their divorce and child custody battle. Agnes is extremely intelligent, has multiple degrees, and has a successful career. She also did not have a history of mental illness.

To rebuild Agnes' self-esteem, she needed sleep to regain her confidence and build a case to fight for joint decision-making; we worked on a self-care plan incorporating affirmations and meditation. My client initially fought the process because she didn't believe in the effects of affirmations and meditation. They were just another "thing to do" she didn't have time for. It took some convincing to get her to at least "try it." Two weeks after stating daily affirmations in conjunction with meditation at night before bed, Agnes began to see and feel a difference in her mental state. In conjunction with working with her trauma therapist to heal, Agnes was able to calm her nervous system during triggering encounters with her ex-husband and work with me in preparing her case for family court.

CASE STUDY #3: Healthy Relationships and the Importance of Establishing Boundaries

Suzanne, an emotional abuse survivor and mom of two, chose not to date for three years following her divorce. She decided to focus on the personal development plan we worked on during her divorce coaching sessions to get her life back on track. Suzanne and I created a personal development plan that focused on trauma therapy, finding her identity, rebuilding relationships with family and friends, and self-care.

At the end of three years, Suzanne felt she was at a point in her life where she was ready to trust her instincts and date again. She created a dating profile on two dating sites and began to swipe through prospects. Within two weeks, she met someone she was interested in getting to know. Griffin, vice president of a financial investment firm and divorced father of three, sparked her interest. On their first date, Suzanne was cautious about sharing her interests and what she was seeking in a future partner. She didn't want Griffin to mirror her interests and become "the man" of her dreams.

Griffin was courteous, respectful, and well-mannered. Suzanne took a chance after three months of dating and decided to have an exclusive relationship with Griffin. By month four, cracks began to appear in their relationship. The courteous, respectful, well-mannered man subtly began to overly criticize the clothes Suzanne wore and the way she wore her hair. He also began to demand a lot of Suzanne's time and complained when she spent time with friends.

The changes in Griffin's behavior got to the point that Suzanne felt uncomfortable expressing how it made her feel. She felt butterflies at the thought of telling Griffin that his words made her uneasy. Suzanne also didn't want to jump to conclusions on Griffin's character since she knew she was still triggered by certain behaviors due to her marriage. Suzanne began to inform her close friends about what Griffin was saying to her to get their thoughts. Her friends were shocked by the statements Griffin made to Suzanne, validating her intuition.

Suzanne began to analyze her relationship with Griffin and the signs, if any, she missed during their initial three months of dating. What she began to realize was that she missed one important aspect of healing during her three years of self-development and discovery. She never learned what a healthy relationship looked like. She worked on herself, repairing the emotional and physical damage of her marriage, but she neglected to learn how to have healthy relationships going forward.

Suzanne also did not establish healthy boundaries with Griffin. She didn't communicate to Griffin during their initial dating stage that she wanted to be treated with kindness, feel heard, and acknowledged when expressing her feelings. She was not transparent with Griffin in the beginning, and now she was at a point in their relationship where she felt uncomfortable expressing herself.

Suzanne eventually ended the relationship after four months of dating. She made a promise to herself to learn the components of a healthy relationship and to clearly express her boundaries in the early stages of dating. I checked in with Suzanne six months after she ended her relationship with Griffin. She had incorporated self-care into her daily routine, was seeing her trauma therapist monthly, and spending time with family and friends. She also had a new friend in her life, but without rushing into a relationship; instead, she chose to focus on enjoying the time they spent together, getting to know each other. Suzanne is not only surviving after rebuilding her life but thriving in her new life.

"You may not control all the events that happen to you, but you can decide not to be reduced by them."

–Maya Angelou